DOWN		B	B	B	B	C	B	A	B	B	A	B	B	A
		8.16 a.m. Cleethorpes Sheffield (Diesel)	6.40 a.m. from King's Cross	To Leicester (London Road)		E.C.S. to Hull (Dairycoates)	To Leeds		To Lincoln (Diesel)	To Skegness	To Leeds and Bradford	To Grimsby	To Derby	9.43 a.m. from Cleethorpes Manchester (London Road)
		280	788	1874	5404	5212	3030	800	798	208	950	192	786	294
					HX	Q		HC ♠		ThO	HC ♠			
		am	am	am	am	am	am	am	am	am	am	am	am	am
KING'S CROSS dep	1							8 20			8 50			
Finsbury Park arr	2							FL			FL			
dep	3													
Greenwood	4							8 34			9 5			
Potters Bar	5													
Brookmans Park	6													
HATFIELD arr	7													
dep	8							8 42			9 13			
Welwyn Garden City arr	9													
dep	10													
Welwyn North	11													
Woolmer Green	12													
Knebworth	13													
Langley Jn.	14													
Stevenage	15													
HITCHIN arr	16							8 56½						
dep	17							8 58			9 26½			
Cadwell	18													
Three Counties	19													
Arlesey	20													
Biggleswade	21													
Sandy	22							9 8½			9 35½			
Tempsford	23													
St. Neots	24													
Offord	25													
HUNTINGDON NORTH arr	26							9 22						
dep	27							9 24			9 48			
Abbots Ripton	28													
Connington South	29													
Holme	30							[4]			[3]			
Yaxley	31		←											
Peterborough East	32			9 24										
PETERBOROUGH NORTH arr	33		9 12	9 28				9 46						
dep	34		9 24	9 30				9 50		9 57	10 7	10 10		
Westwood Jn.	35													
Werrington Jn.	36		9 31					9 56½		10 4	10 12	10 18		
Tallington	37													
Essendine	38		9c45					10 3½			10 20½			
Little Bytham	39		9 53											
Corby Glen	40			B				[1]						
Stoke	41		10 6					10 14½			10 32			
Great Ponton	42			10.3 a.m. Sheffield Hull				[2]			[2]			
GRANTHAM arr	43		10 14					10 22						
dep	44							10 26	10 31		10 39		10 55	
Barkston South Jn.	45							10 31½	10 37½		10 42½			
Hougham	46			5214										
Claypole	47													
NEWARK NORTH GATE arr	48							10 41						
dep	49							10 43			10 51½			
Crow Park	50													
Tuxford North Jn.	51										[4]			
RETFORD arr	52	10 5						11 2½						11 19
dep	53	10 25						11 5			11 12½			11 23
Ranskill	54													
Bawtry	55							[7]			[7]			
Rossington	56													
Black Carr Jn.	57													
DONCASTER arr	58			10 48				11 32			11 39½			
dep	59			11 5	11 5	11†12	11 15				11 46			
Carcroft & Adwick	60						11 22							
Adwick Jn.	61						11 24				11 53			
Arksey Loop	62													
Shaftholme Jn.	63				11 13									
Knottingley	64													
Balne	65				11 21									
Heck	66				11 25									
Temple Hirst	67				11 31									
SELBY arr	68				11 38									
dep	69				11 40									
Riccall	70													
YORK arr	71				12 1									
dep	72													

788: Calls Tallington on ThO for staff purposes

208: From 17th July to 28th August inclusive

1874: Conveys portion off 8.0 a.m. from Kings Cross

DOWN		A	B	B	A	B	A	B	A	B	A	A	A	A	A	C	B
		To Newcastle (Tyne Commission Quay)		To Sheffield	To Edinburgh	To Cleethorpes	To Newcastle	To Yarmouth Beach	9.15 a.m. Cambridge to Manchester Cen. MFO, Sheffield Vic. MFXQ	To Boston (Diesel)	To Lincoln (Diesel)	9.30 a.m. Liverpool (Central) Hull	8.0 a.m. Parkeston Quay to Liverpool Cen.	To Edinburgh	7.20 a.m. Colchester Newcastle	11.53 a.m. E.C.S. from Pyewipe Jn.	To Derby
		40	1812	474	42	315	44	1807	508	880	802	78	510	50	46	800	830
		HC MWThO ♠			HC ♠	HC	HC ♠		MFO MFXQ			HC		HC ♠	HC	MXQ	
		am	am	am	am	PM	am	am	PM	am	am	PM	PM	am	PM	PM	am
KING'S CROSS dep	1	9 5			9 30		9 40							10 0			
Finsbury Park arr	2	FL			FL		FL							FL			
dep	3																
Greenwood	4	9 19			9 45		9 54							10 15			
Potters Bar	5																
Brookmans Park	6																
HATFIELD arr	7																
dep	8	9 27			9 53		10 2							10 23			
Welwyn Garden City arr	9																
dep	10																
Welwyn North	11																
Woolmer Green	12																
Knebworth	13																
Langley Jn.	14																
Stevenage	15																
HITCHIN arr	16																
dep	17	9 39½			10 6½		10 14½							10 36½			
Cadwell	18																
Three Counties	19																
Arlesey	20																
Biggleswade	21																
Sandy	22	9 48			10 15½		10 23							10 45½			
Tempsford	23																
St. Neots	24						[2]										
Offord	25																
HUNTINGDON NORTH arr	26																
dep	27	9 59½			10 28		10 36½							10 58			
Abbots Ripton	28																
Connington South	29																
Holme	30	[5]			[2]		[3]							[3]			
Yaxley	31																
Peterborough East	32		10 23														
PETERBOROUGH NORTH arr	33		10 28														
dep	34	10 19½			10 46		10 54½	10 58						11 17			
Westwood Jn.	35																
Werrington Jn.	36	10 24			10 51		10 59							11 22			
Tallington	37						[1]										
Essendine	38	10 31			10 59½		11 7							11 30½			
Little Bytham	39																
Corby Glen	40						[1]										
Stoke	41	10 41			11 11		11 18							11 42			
Great Ponton	42	[1]												[2]			
GRANTHAM arr	43						11 23½										
dep	44	10 46½			11 16		11 29½			11 35	11 41			11 49			
Barkston South Jn.	45	10 50			11 19½		11 35			11 41½	11 49			11 52½			
Hougham	46	[3]															
Claypole	47																
NEWARK NORTH GATE arr	48				11 28½		11 43½										
dep	49	11 1½												12 1½			
Crow Park	50						[2]										
Tuxford North Jn.	51	[5]												[2]			
RETFORD arr	52																
dep	53	11 23		11 40	11 45½		12 2		12 6				12 14	12 20½			
Ranskill	54																
Bawtry	55	[7]			[2]		[5]							[6]			
Rossington	56																
Black Carr Jn.	57														12 24	12	
DONCASTER arr	58						12 24½					12 23			12 32	12	
dep	59	11 46½			12 4	12 16	12 28½					12 37		12 43½	12 46		
Carcroft & Adwick	60																
Adwick Jn.	61				[3]		[2]							[2]	[4]		
Arksey Loop	62																
Shaftholme Jn.	63	11 51			12 12		12 37							12 50	12 58		
Knottingley	64																
Balne	65																
Heck	66																
Temple Hirst	67																
SELBY arr	68														1 13½		
dep	69	12 3½			12 25		12 49½							1 3	1 15½		
Riccall	70																
YORK arr	71	12U20					1 6								1 36		
dep	72	12 27			12 40		1 11							1 18½	1 43		

40: Runs WThO to 3rd Sept. incl. and MO 23rd June to 8th September inclusive

44: Conveys portion for Tyne Commission Quay on Mondays and Wednesdays until 27th August, also on Wednesday 10th September, Thursdays 4th and 11th September and Friday 12th September

508, 510: Retford "Straight Line"

C000277799

BRITISH RAILWAYS
EASTERN REGION
STAFF RAILWAY SOCIETY

BRITISH RAILWAYS
EASTERN REGION
STAFF RAILWAY SOCIETY

BRITISH RAILWAYS
EASTERN REGION
STAFF RAILWAY SOCIETY

EASTERN REGION STEAM TWILIGHT

PART ONE

BRITISH RAILWAYS
EASTERN REGION
STAFF RAILWAY SOCIETY

BRITISH RAILWAYS
EASTERN REGION
STAFF RAILWAY SOCIETY

BRITISH RAILWAYS
EASTERN REGION
STAFF RAILWAY SOCIETY

1 *The Kings Cross A4 No 60007 'Sir Nigel Gresley' in the hands of Driver William Hoole was a formidable combination. Here, immaculately turned out for working the Stephenson Locomotive Society's 'Golden Jubilee Special' it waits to leave Kings Cross for its high speed sprint to Doncaster on 23rd May 1959.*

EASTERN REGION STEAM TWILIGHT

Part One
South of Grantham

Colin Walker

PENDYKE PUBLICATIONS

INTRODUCTION

In common with my books on the last years of the Great Central main line this is another personal collection of photographic reminiscences concentrating on the Eastern Region of British Railways during its final period of steam operation.

It is not a comprehensive record of the last locomotive types at work in the region but is more the result of days, half days, nights and sometimes even the odd few minutes spent with a camera beside Eastern Region tracks or on Eastern Region engines. If it reveals a bias towards the larger locomotive types it does so because they were of particular personal inspiration.

Following a brief look in at Liverpool Street and the Great Eastern section during the reign of the 'Britannias' and the last of the N7 tanks the book then moves to Kings Cross and its environs before taking the G.N. main line down to Grantham. A lengthy stop is made at Peterborough and brief digressions are made into March, Norwich and onto the High Dyke ironstone branch.

Some of the weather conditions I encountered were grim to say the least. A visit to March took place on a bleak day in Winter when a cloud-obscured sun struggled desperately to lift both the temperature and the gloom only to give up early in the afternoon. However, to me, steam trains were wonderful to watch in any light and what was lost in detail or sharpness was often more than made up for in atmosphere and dramatic effect.

As with many of my books I have included some shots of enginemen because they were a special breed and men of great character. Whether they were élite top link main line crews or movers of coal and ironstone they were a pleasure to know and each possessed their own special expertise. It was to steam enginemen that I owe some of the most enjoyable moments of my life. Many have now passed on but they are still remembered with immense gratitude.

Also warmly acknowledged were the facilities and assistance officially provided by the Eastern Region of British Railways and unofficially by numerous individual members of railway staff who aided and abetted so many of my inspired but harmless transgressions. Without their connivance a large number of these photographs would never have been taken.

Copyright Colin Walker and Pendyke Publications.

Published 1990

Pendyke Publications,
'Gorffwysfa'
Methodist Hill,
Froncysyllte,
Llangollen,
Clwyd.
LL20 7SN

ISBN 0 904318 13 3

Typesetting by KC Graphics, Shrewsbury.

Printed by the Amadeus Press Ltd., Huddersfield, W. Yorkshire

2 *The reign of the 'Britannia' Pacifics on the Great Eastern section. At Liverpool Street No 70039 'Sir Christopher Wren' stands with a good head of steam awaiting departure time with the 5.30pm express to Norwich and Cromer. 7.6.58.*

3 *Romance did not appear to be much in evidence on a gloomy St. Valentine's day in 1959 when this photograph of No 70006 'Robert Burns' was taken at Liverpool St. as it rested at the buffer stops after bringing in an evening express from Norwich.*

4 *On the last day of May 1958 No 70034 'Thomas Hardy' stands impatient to depart from Liverpool Street with the 5.30pm to Norwich.*

Following pages. **5** *On the same day the camera distracts the attention of the train spotters as it catches No 70008 'Black Prince' pulling out of Liverpool Street with the down 'Broadsman'.*

1 The legendary Liverpool Street pilots. J69 No 68619 and N5 No 69614 stand at the centre road resplendent with their high gloss paintwork, burnished steel and polished brass and copper work. During a period when labour in urban and industrial areas was scarce and too precious to use on engine cleaning it was an uplifting experience to see these two engines maintained in such splendid condition. Like the liveried J72 tanks on the North Eastern Region at York and Newcastle these two Liverpool St. pilots were evidence of some inspired leadership and not a few hard stressed city commuters found a moment at rush hours to stop and admire them thus proving their undoubted public relations value. 31.5.58.

8 No 70035 Rudyard Kipling gets the green light and prepares to leave Platform 10 with an express for Clacton. 14.2.59.

tanks their last regular work. These robust and compactly built tank engines with Walscharts valve gear and piston valves all tucked inside the frames were both quick off the mark and possessed a fine turn of speed. Like their counterparts on the G.N., the N2s, they seemed ideally suited to the work they did. Here, No 69632, one of the short travel valve engines, sets off from North Woolwich on the 9th September 1961 with the 10am train which terminated at Stratford Low Level.

9 On the same day one of the long travel valve members of the class, No 69686, rounds the curve at Fork Junction, Stratford with a train to North Woolwich.

10 N7 No 69725 in a most grimy state and working out its last days rounds Fork Junction at Stratford Low Level with a train for North Woolwich.

11 On April 6th 1961 with the kind permission of Richard Hardy, the District Motive Power Superintendent, I spent the day riding N7s on the North Woolwich trains. For the first part of the day I was in the care of Driver Alf Bennett who was in charge of long travel valve engine No 69675. During a brief station stop he is seen in deep dimensional conversation with Bill Lockwood, the Locomotive Inspector who accompanied me. Was this the size of the one that got

12 *No 69675 gets under way with a rapid acceleration as Alf Bennett winds up the gear and shortens the cut-off.*

13 *No 69675 heading a train for North Woolwich pauses at West Green with its Westinghouse pump panting away. The service from Palace Gates has long been discontinued and much of the route as far as Stratford has now been buried under road and housing developments.*

14 *Another stylish hard runner was Kings Cross driver Ted Hailstone whose regular engine was A4 Pacific No 60014 'Silver Link' seen here standing quiescent after arriving with the up 'White Rose'. 14.2.59.*

KINGS CROSS

Kings Cross and its environs was arguably the most exciting of all the London main line terminals and perhaps nowhere were the many moods of a steam locomotive so vividly displayed.

From the calm tranquility of the buffer stop area where engines stood at rest after completing their journeys to the impatient north end where an impetuous, wheel-spinning start was often a prelude to the measured departure of a down express. Having carefully threaded its way over the pointwork to one of the portals of Gasworks tunnel first engine and then train would disappear into a bouquet of smoke and steam. Such were the officially permitted spectacles enjoyed by throngs of train spotters over many generations.

To those with a good A to Z guide and a more restless and daring temperate however, there were other possibilities. One was a high risk flit through Kings Cross goods depot and yard with detection threatened at every turn. Another involved a brisk hike around the depressed Dickensian back streets west of the Caledonian Road, followed by a furtive dash alongside the North London line and a final scramble down into the G.N. cutting. Both choices of route led to a photographer's paradise. This was the open stretch of line between the Gasworks and Copenhagen tunnels wherein was crammed the signal boxes of Belle Isle and Copenhagen Junction, the outlet and entry to Kings Cross engine shed and goods yard and the impressive high level bridge by which the North London line made its crossing. The whole scene was overviewed by the stark watchword EBONITE scripted on a nearby and particularly evil factory chimney concealed within its own tall brick tower which boasted small dormer windows in its tapered top stage.

This was a very busy section of railway where movements were compound, complex, and because of the concealing tunnels, sometimes quite sudden. One was always on guard in case of discovery and challenge while being equally alert to matters of personal safety. With such priorities firmly in mind one could then devote some attention to photography.

One of the most exciting facets of the tunnel exit from Kings Cross was the transformation that could overcome an engine between its nonchalant disappearance into Gasworks tunnel on the way from the shed to the station and its re-emergence a short while later with a string of well filled coaches on its hook. The outcome could never be predicted but the sounds from within the tunnel usually provided an indication because once inside the bore engines would come to grips with a gradient of 1 in 107. The regulator would be fully opened and cut-off adjusted as they battled up the climb to Finsbury Park where the incline eased a little.

With steam still moist and many fires only just beginning to burn through, those Pacifics and V2s could become wonderfully extrovert monsters bursting with energy as they announced its release to the skies. They were a heart stirring sight and occasionally so awesome that one had real difficulty in concentrating on the business of photography with a large and extremely manual plate camera.

Of course, the G.N. main line's 'solo' tradition out of Kings Cross always ensured a good quota of pyrotechnic displays because under normal circumstances assistance was neither sought nor offered by the engine at the rear of the train that had previously worked the empty stock into the terminus. Faint hearted customs like banking and double heading might be all right on the load-conscious London Midland Region but it offended the independent spirit of the average Eastern Region crew. After all, had they not traditionally enjoyed the benefits of a 'big engine' policy which gave them a sense of mastery over the loads they hauled?

In addition to the nervous excitement of photographing round the tunnels, Kings Cross was associated for me with a number of other highly charged episodes. It was at the engine shed one summer afternoon where in order to obtain some high level shots of the depot I climbed one of the tall floodlights near the coaling plant. After some precarious firings of the shutter from the cramped, swaying maintenance platform near the top my anxiety to descend from the horrors of vertigo had to be swiftly curbed. For at least 15 minutes I had to remain 'frozen' while an efficient railway policeman down below at the front of the shed recorded the names of some hapless schoolboys who had been too absorbed spotting to realise the danger. As a school teacher my name in his book would have been a rich prize indeed and

would surely have exposed some of the rotting timbers of our education system!

I also have keen footplate memories of Kings Cross like squatting down on the floor just inside the tender corridor and behind the firmly closed cab doors of A4 No 60007 'Sir Nigel Gresley' at the head of a night sleeper to Newcastle. With the rain drooling down the back of my neck I was forced to make a close study of the boots and overalls of Driver Bill Hoole and his fireman who were tightly squeezed against the doors so that they effectively prevented any glimpses onto the footplate. This became urgently necessary when 'authority' appeared down below at the platform end to issue them with instructions and 'chat'. The concealment was remarkably thorough but oh, how I longed for the departure that would release me from such tense and liquid discomfort and what a relief when it came and I was able to rise from the coal dust slurry I was sitting in and assume a more dignified posture in the fireman's seat.

Bill Hoole was an incredible character. His straight faced humour, his penchant for high speed, his scant adherence to some of the rules and regulations, his refusal to carry a watch and his tendency to burn coal did not always endear him to the management. He was nevertheless an excellent railwayman and together with a number of his Kings Cross colleagues he helped to put the East Coast Main Line back in the vanguard of British express train running in the 1950s with those splendid Pacifics.

Correspondence with Bill was always amusing. His handwriting was self-consciously small and very much part of his wit. He rejoiced in describing the occasions when magnifying glasses had to be employed by recipients of his letters and cards to make them readable.

All my footplate trips with him were memorable. At one time it would be flailing along through the early hours of a morning in high summer in 1958 with speed well in the eighties on No 60821, a run-down, off beat V2 which had been substituted for the booked Pacific. It was heading the down 'Tynesider'. With the smoke and coal dust swirling round the cab and caking the eyes and nostrils we positively stormed up Stoke bank overtaking in the early daybreak A4 No 60028 on a down parcels train which had been relegated to the slow line to let us pass.

Its driver, Charlie Huggins of Kings Cross No 2 link and a colleague of Bills, eyed us in consternation as we passed and vehemently stabbed a gesture of colourful protest at our furious progress. Then, later, when the two men met up in the loco crews' cabin at Grantham he was moved to announce an outspoken verdict with the words "That man is bloody mad". Perhaps a trifle strong but we all knew what he meant!

Equally thrilling on another occasion was a run up from Grantham again with Bill's own A4 'Sir Nigel Gresley' heading the overnight car sleeper from Perth. With 18 on we swept down Stoke bank touching 105 and converted a late start from Grantham into an early arrival in London. Passengers in the sleeping cars still had over an hour to enjoy their slumbers but these had obviously been disturbed because within minutes of rolling to rest at the buffer stops the carriage doors opened and a group of passengers of both genders, many in dressing gowns, clustered round the engine to look with drowsy curiosity and glazed amusement at its driver and fireman. One can only imagine that they had experienced some difficulty remaining in their bunks on the way down Stoke bank!

How delightful that his many 'sins' at the regulator should have been so generously forgiven when shortly before his retirement he was selected with No 60007 to haul the Stephenson Locomotive Society's Golden Jubilee special train and honoured with an officially approved, (though constrained!) 112 mph down Stoke bank. That superb run is also remembered in this book.

No memories of Kings Cross would be complete without recalling those nights spent during the shed's last year taking long exposures of engines being lined up for duty after being serviced and prepared in the dark hours. Thanks to the unofficial co-operation and complicity of Ron Dwight, the night foreman, I was able to obtain some privileged shots of the end of a proud tradition before it disappeared for ever. How eloquently those quiet routines and nocturnally subdued movements portrayed an industry that never ever slept but where life was always astir.

15 A 'gambler's' photograph taken through the smoke-fogged window at the top of the stairs leading to the Civil Engineers offices looks down onto the arrival platforms where V2 no 60950 and A1 Pacific No 60148 'Aboyeur' take a break after bringing in expresses from Newcastle and Leeds respectively. Through the arch a Sulzer Type 2 diesel No D5065 has worked in the empty stock of a down express.

16 At 8.20 on the raw night of February 14th 1959 a Leeds Copley Hill A1 No 60131 'Osprey' waits patiently for the empty stock of the up 'Queen of Scots' Pullman to be removed so that it can retire to 'top shed' for refreshment.

10 ... train at Kings Cross heading an evening special chartered by the Lincolnshire Standard newspaper. Because of the removal of water troughs and cranes No 4472, for a time, hauled an extra tender. It is perhaps difficult to realise now what a tonic it was when this classic engine emerged in its pre-war apple green livery and with the Doncaster 'smile' on its smokebox door unsullied by those unsightly smoke deflectors and Midland style number and shed plates. It is also ironic that out of a class of 78 engines No 4472 was the only example of these magnificent engines to survive, though Driver Norman McKilliop's 'Spearmint' in the Scottish Region nearly made it until it was discovered to have a cracked frame.

11 No 60007 Sir Nigel Gresley again bursts out of Copenhagen tunnel at the head of an afternoon express to Newcastle. Compared with the previous picture its external condition indicates that it is coming up for a major overhaul at Doncaster works.

Previous pages

19 A very spruce A3 No 60044 'Melton' sets off from Kings Cross with the 5.5 pm train for Cambridge, 18.4.62

20 An overcast morning on August 14th 1961 the down 'Tees-Thames' express moves out of Kings Cross headed by No 60013 'Dominion of New Zealand'

21 An A1 Pacific No 60147 'North Eastern' threads its way over the crossovers and prepares to enter Gasworks Tunnel with the down 'Queen of Scots Pullman'

22 On September 8th 1961 a great East Coast main line steam tradition came to an end when the world speed record holder, A4 Pacific 60022 'Mallard', set off from Kings Cross with the last down 'Elizabethan'. Here she is climbing out of Gasworks Tunnel at the start of her 392 mile non stop run to Edinburgh.

opening of Kings Cross station this gap between the two tunnels was the site of the Great Northern's temporary terminus at Maiden Lane from 1850 to 1852. Behind the B1 can be seen the one time Kings Cross Cemetery Station. Opened in 1861 it combined the functions of mortuary and funeral station from where coffins and mourners were transported by rail to Colney Hatch, (now New Southgate), where a cemetery of 150 acres was operated by the Great Northern London Cemetery Company. Whether or not the stirring sounds of Sturrock and Stirling Singles climbing lustily past with down expresses had a disturbing effect on some of the corpses is not known but by 1873 the Cemetery Station had closed and the building remained empty and derelict until its demolition in 1961. It was replaced by a ready-mixed concrete depot.

25 *Drifting downhill without effort is a Kings Cross A3 No 60061 'Pretty Polly' heading for Gasworks Tunnel and the terminus with an express from Hull and Doncaster. 1.6.63.*

light work of the climb past Belle Isle with the 6.12pm express to Leeds. On the right is the line giving access to Kings Cross shed and yard. 1.6.63.

26 Against the collar. An A4 No 60033 'Seagull' climbs with determination past Belle Isle with the 9.40am down boat train from Kings Cross to Newcastle Tyne Commission Quay.

27 An A1 Pacific No 60139 'Sea Eagle' lifts the 6.36pm express to Doncaster up the gradient towards Copenhagen tunnel.

Following pages.

28 Unkempt but on time. Coasting under the North London line bridge a New England A2 No 60520 'Owen Tudor' approaches journey's end with a boat train from Newcastle Tyne Commission Quay.

29 An up express from Hull and Doncaster drifts down the gradient past Belle Isle signal box with A4 No 60034 'Lord Faringdon' in charge.

30 *Shortly after being fitted with a Kylchap exhaust, double chimney and small deflector shields, an A3 Pacific No 60055 'Woolwinder' backs out of Copenhagen Tunnel on its way to the terminus* [...]

31 *A York A2 Pacific No 60524 'Herringbone' passes Belle Isle with a down summer relief to York and Scarborough* [...]

34 The storm after the lull. Following 'Green Arrow's placid reversal into the terminus to collect the down 'Scarborough Flyer' I was not prepared for the sequel that ensued. With that incomparably thrilling Gresley three cylinder roar here she is throwing everything into a supreme effort as she accelerates up the climb to Holloway with the heavily loaded train. Taking photographs like this was not good for the nerves and it was quite a few moments before I recovered from what was a quite overwhelming experience. Was the G.N. main line's 'solo' tradition ever better displayed that this?!

terminus to take over the down 'Scarborough Flyer' the prototype V2 No 60800 'Green Arrow' drifts under the North London line bridge and passes Belle Isle box. The supply of coal on the tender seems to be of rather mixed quality. 12.8.61.

A4 No 60034 'Lord Faringdon' pauses beneath the North London line overbridge before moving into the shed yard.

35 *Sounds from within the high level bore of Copenhagen Tunnel which led directly into Kings Cross shed and goods yard announces the arrival of York's most 'local' engine, V2 No 60847 'St. Peter's School, York' which is making for 'top shed' after working in a freight to Hornsey Yard.*

36 *A Leeds Copley Hill A1 No 60133 'Pommern' makes a splendid climb under the North London line with the 10.20am down Leeds express. 8.9.61.*

37 The 'Scotsman' Rules, O.K.? Five years after the official end of steam out of Kings Cross sees Alan Pegler's preserved A3 No 4472 'Flying Scotsman' making a massive climb under the North London line bridge with a Locomotive Club of Great Britain special to Hull via Boston on September 21st 1968.

38 With the sun high overhead a Grantham A3 No 60108 'Gay Crusader' attacks the gradient as it approaches Copenhagen Junction box with a down Leeds express. The climb through Gasworks Tunnel must have been a 'pea-souper' because dense fumes and vapours are still clearing from within the wheels and frames creating a strange haze around the engine.

39 A3 Pacific No 60047 'Donovan' heads a down morning Leeds express under the North London line and approaches Copenhagen tunnel.

40 Passing the same spot is Leeds Copley Hill A1 No 60141 'Abbotsford' with the up 'White Rose'.

BRITISH RAILWAYS
MANURE TRAFFIC.

NOTICE IS HEREBY GIVEN THAT ANY PERSON
OR PERSONS LOADING IN TO THE COMPANY'S
WAGONS FISH. OFFAL. ANIMAL MATTER DECAYED
VEGETABLES. OR ANY OTHER REFUSE LIKELY
TO CREATE A NUISANCE WILL BE PROSECUTED.

BY ORDER.

41 *An unequivocal notice that appeared near one of the unofficial accesses to Kings Cross loco*

Top Shed

42 *An engine crew studs outside the main line running shed finds A1 Pacific No 60132 'Marmion'*

line up of engines. From left to right is A1 No 60139 'Sea Eagle', a 9F 2-10-0, A2 No 60500 'Edward Thompson', A1 No 60120 'Kittiwake', V2 No 60928 and A4 No 60017 'Silver Fox'. 1.6.63.

lowering of the tonal scale meant that detail became very subtle. Taken on a long exposure outside the main line running shed are A3s Nos 60062 'Minoru', 60061 'Pretty Polly' and A4 No 60021 'Wild Swan'. 18.4.63.

60128 'Bongrace'. 18.4.63.

Faringdon' and 60021 'Wild Swan'.

49 Night Companions. In the early hours of the morning A3 Pacifics Nos 60066 'Merry Hampton' and 60107 'Royal Lancer' stand inside the main line running shed at Kings Cross ready for duty.

60007 'Sir Nigel Gresley' – obviously a proud possession. and A1 Pacific No 60153 'Borderer'.

50 A4 Pacific No 60034 'Lord Faringdon'. 1.30am.

51 Out of steam and under repair A3 No 60061 'Pretty Polly' stands inside the main line running shed.

Following pages, Kings Cross Characters.

52 Driver Bill Hoole in his element at the regulator of A4 Pacific No 60007 'Sir Nigel Gresley'.

Though he had a reputation for pushing his engines hard there was nothing crude or hamfisted about Bill Hoole's methods. This photograph taken during an impeccable start south from Doncaster with not a trace of a slip shows a driver completely in tune with his engine. Sitting alert and poised in his seat, his right hand grasps the regulator which is not yet fully open, while his left hand holds the handle of the reversing gear. By the smallest adjustments to both controls 'Sir Nigel' is being worked into speed without any strain. The fireworks will come later!

53 Another Kings Cross character in casual working uniform. Locomotive Inspector George Harland with Doncaster driver Stan Holgate on the footplate of A4 Pacific No 60021 'Wild Swan'. 18.4.63.

54 *Entry . . . A shot from the cab of A4 Pacific No 60021 'Wild Swan' as it climbs past Copenhagen Junction signal box and prepares to dive into the tunnel with the 8.10am from Kings Cross to Doncaster and Hull. 18.4.63.*

55 . . . and exit.   *An Edinburgh Haymarket A4 No 60009 'Union of South Africa' bursts out of Copenhagen tunnel with the down non-stop 'Elizabethan' in August 1961. No 60009 was the last A4 to receive a major overhaul at Doncaster works in November 1963.*

56 At the north end of Copenhagen Tunnel, traffic and light engines making for Kings Cross yard and shed were carried over the main lines to the 'high level' tunnel on the down side on a flyover. Here, climbing beneath the flyover with the 9.40am boat train from Kings Cross to Newcastle Tyne Commission Quay is A4 No 60003 'Andrew K. McKosh'. 14.8.61.

57 A3 No 60044 'Melton' drifts down the hill into Copenhagen tunnel with the 9.16am express from York to Kings Cross.

58 Woefully neglected and near the end of its days A3 No 60062 'Minoru' climbs the bank

59 Coasting under the Caledonian Road bridge is A4 No 60008 'Dwight D. Eisenhower' with the

61 In the second photograph 'Silver Fox' heading the 6.26pm down express to Doncaster and Hull is locked in battle with a Brush Type 3 diesel on a local to Hitchin. At this point the diesel was having slightly the better of the tussle but after Finsbury Park it would be a different matter.

first it is seen making light work of the climb to Holloway top with a down express for Doncaster and Hull while overtaking A1 No 60141 'Abbotsford' which is climbing alongside with the down evening York parcels. No 60017's driver offers a thumbs up greeting.

arranged exhaust makes a strong departure from Holloway car loading dock with the 7.56am Anglo-Scottish Car Carrier.

Holloway Bank with the 7.45am express from Leeds to Kings Cross.

64 The 10.10am express from Kings Cross to Leeds and Bradford emerges from beneath the flyover with a Doncaster shedded A2 Pacific No 60520 'Owen Tudor' obviously well in control. 14.8.61.

In 1965 shortly before the end of steam working out of Kings Cross an A4 on 60026 'Miles Beevor' climbs to Holloway top with a down express.

A3 'Flying Fox' No 60035 'Persimmon' is obviously in good fettle internally as she climbs past Holloway with a clearing exhaust, 'sanders operating and a 'white feather' showing at the safety valves. The train is an evening relief to Newcastle. The 'period' building behind the train was formerly the Islington Electric Light Company's power station.

67 A last minute hitch with the booked A4 sees a typically soot covered York A1 No 60154 'Bon Accord' heading the down 'Flying Scotsman' up Holloway Bank on 14th August 1961.

Hadley Wood Tunnel an A3 No 60040 'Cameronian' still with its single chimney is getting well into its stride past the site of the former Greenwood signal box with the 6.20pm express from Kings Cross to Leeds. 22.5.59.

70 *And after. Another A1 No 60144 'Kings Courier' speeds northwards with a down sleeping car express. 22.5.59.*

No 60130 'Kestrel' cruises past Greenwood signal box at Hadley Wood with the down 'Harrogate Sunday Pullman'.

71 A V2 No 60852 on the main line romps towards the newly opened tunnel at Hadley Wood

72 A1 No 60135 'Madge Wildfire' hustles through Hadley Wood station with a down Newcastle

B1 4-6-0s had charge of the Kings Cross-Cleethorpes expresses. In this photograph an unidentified member of the class heads north from Hadley Wood Tunnel towards Potters Bar with the 6.45pm from Kings Cross. 22.5.59.

black mark against the depot and a comment on the acute staff shortages it suffered. An infamous examples was No 60154 'Bon Accord' seen here speeding driverless near Potters Bar with a down evening Newcastle express. Judging by the 'white feather' showing at the safety valves her boiler had no difficulty in generating steam. August 1961.

75 A1 No 60119 'Patrick Stirling' nears the top of the climb out of London at Potters Bar with a down express to Leeds.

76 The day's work is virtually over for the fireman of A4 Pacific No 60017 'Silver Fox' and he is able to take life easily in his seat as his engine coasts through the station at Potters Bar on its way

PASSENGERS CROSS
THE LINE BY THE
SUBWAY ONLY

77 *In a steady downpour a New England V2 No 60924 draws to a halt at Hitchin with the 4.19pm semi-fast from Kings Cross to Peterborough, April 1958.*

78 *During April 1958 V2 No 60800 'Green Arrow' was afflicted by steaming problems and after receiving attention at 'top shed' it was put on the 5pm semi-fast from Kings Cross to Peterborough to check its performance. This photograph taken from the cab shows the engine held on the slow line at Everton box between Sandy and Tempsford to allow the down 'Yorkshire Pullman' to overtake on the main line.*

Following pages

79 *Running proud. 'Silver Fox' again, this time outward bound from Kings Cross, is caught pushing up the speed near Potters Bar with a down Newcastle express. Her gear is pulled well up and she is running very economically on a short cut off, full regulator and with steam to spare.*

Cross to Peterborough. April 1963.

ahead of time as it nears Fletton sidings south of Peterborough with the 9.8am express from Hull and Doncaster to Kings Cross. 18.8.62.

PETERBOROUGH

In steam days when passengers were settling into their journeys from Kings Cross and were being whisked over Stilton Fen and past the landscape of brick fields and kiln chimneys that marked the exit from the erstwhile county of Huntingdon they would both feel and hear the brakes begin to bite as their train was dragged down in speed from a mile a minute plus.

Rumbling over rail and river between heavy bridge girders, past power station, carriage sidings, premises and properties they would pass beneath a fine bowstring bridge to make a very deferential passage through a decidedly mean and nondescript station composed of shabby buildings and cramped platforms. Once clear, those passengers looking out on the up side would then be treated to a large acreage of marshalling yards and a sizeable engine shed as their train gathered speed again.

For southbound trains the change in tempo was even more drastic because passengers had just enjoyed the exhileration of a whirlwind sprint down the long 18 mile bank from Stoke tunnel up in the limestone country of South Lincolnshire. After reaching speeds in the high ranges which might even have nudged three figures they too would find their progress grinding down to little more than cycling pace as the engine on the front clanked its way through the dog's leg track formation that accompanied the station's architectural blight.

This, of course, was Peterborough where discussions with the city fathers about improving the track arrangements and rebuilding the North Station had grumbled on for decades with no practical solution materialising until well into the 'Deltic' era. To what was after all a cathedral city and an important agricultural and manufacturing centre there is no doubt that the railway facilities up on the main line at Peterborough North were little short of insulting particularly when compared with the commodious station provided at a town like Rugby which at the close of the 19th Century boasted less than half the population of Peterborough and which geographically occupied a similar position on the rival West Coast route. Certainly Peterborough was a constant reminder that the old Great Northern and its successor the L.N.E.R. were not the most prosperous of railway companies and money for such improvements was not so easy to find.

However imperfect its reputation with the travelling public and railway operating staff, Peterborough's blemishes were certainly no deterrent when it came to lineside photography. On the contrary, the fact that trains had to slow down and then start work again was quite an attraction because, in doing so, a number of them produced a display of life from the chimney top.

Locations however were important to me. Rather than the north end where a maze of tracks combined with a veritable forest of signals, poles, posts and a mesh of wires, my preference nearly always took me to the south of the station. Here was the impressive bowstring bridge beyond which the G.N. Main line became simplifed and collected together into four tracks, two up and two down, for the crossing of the Nene bridges and viaduct. For up trains this entailed a short climb at 1 in 237. With no catenary then in place, good visibility, clear signalling and ample audible warning I was perhaps guilty of a somewhat liberal interpretation of my photographing permit when it came to using the bridges and their approaches. Among the girders I found a number of safe refuges at different levels from where I could photograph trains in a rare and dramatic setting.

My eager use of the Nene bridges did not blind me to other interesting viewpoints. One of these was the local power station, at that time a quite modern edifice, which it was impossible to ignore being heftily sited beside both the main line and the river. During my waits for trains I had often eyed its roof top and wondered.

In the end curiosity consumed me and I made contact with the manager in charge of Peterborough's electricity generation and with his kind permission I enjoyed the best part of an hour one Saturday morning behind the roof parapet looking down onto the railway. I should love to have stayed longer but a reasonable limit had to be placed on such a special privilege particularly as a member of the power station staff was assigned to keep me company.

Then there was that other station 'down below' at Peterborough East. It was a piecemeal building but it did possess a charming rural flavour that provided a real appetiser for those cheerful, carefree holiday destinations on the East Anglian coast. Unlike the North station which specialised in prestige expresses with most of them non-stop, here was a meeting place and staging point where leisurely cross country passenger trains to and from the industrial Midlands stopped to change their engines and train crews and where there was time for a good chinwag.

As if to emphasise that trains had reached a gateway to East Anglia many of the engines that took over the eastbound trains still displayed their Great Eastern origins or were types like the B17 4-6-0s whose employment had become confined to depots in the Eastern counties. Their panting Westinghouse pumps announced that railways in this part of the country did some things rather differently.

It was an eager wish to secure some photographs and possibly ride on examples of the B12s, 'Claud Hamiltons' and B17s before they all disappeared to the scrapyard that drew me to Peterborough East, March and to Norwich. The former Great Eastern types with their spacious cabs and pleasant riding qualities were engines of fine character while the Gresley B17s, though hardly sharing the same distinction for a smooth conveyance, were nevertheless of special interest to me. It was the 'Football' variety that had made such an impression on me as a child when, in their apple green days, they added some tremendous spirit and sparkle to the Great Central line expresses particularly over the London Extension. The B17s were a handsome engine and almost to the end were kept in a most creditable external condition by their home depots.

The changes that have taken place at Peterborough since the end of steam have been quite astounding. No longer do the 'main liners' creep through at 25mph but the redesigned track layout and the rebuilt North station now sees the non-stops flashing through 'under the wires' at 105.

Also, with its lines to Rugby and Northampton long since closed and abandoned the town now only just clings to its reputation as a railway cross roads and it is a staggered one at that. It continues to be so by virtue of the former Midland line from Leicester and Melton Mowbray which always did provide a strong source of cross country traffice between the Midlands and Eastern England. However, its passenger trains no longer wander down to the East station to change engines and 'pass the time' because that station has also disappeared and all east-west services are now dealt with at the re-modelled North station. It all makes better sense but what a fascinating and colourful chapter has been closed.

Peterborough East, March and Norwich

82 *A D16/3 No 62529 stands in the homely surroundings of Peterborough East with a platform each side waiting to leave with the 4.38pm through train to Harwich.*

sided at Spital Bridge) await departure time from Peterborough
East with the 3.50pm train to Northampton.

to hand over as train to a London Midland 4F from Rowley shed No 44237. This photograph makes an interesting comment on the different
motive power resources of the Eastern and London Midland Regions at the time. The Eastern Region with its generous supply of large express
passenger engines and abundance of capable mixed traffic types rarely had difficulty in providing adequate and appropriate power for its
regular services. The London Midland on the other hand often had to resort to the use of freight engines many of which were of dubious
suitability. 18.8.62.

85 *Eastwards from Peterborough East. One of the attractions of the East station was the appearance of engine types identified only with the Eastern Counties and the former Great Eastern Railway. In this photograph a former Great Eastern 'Claud Hamilton' 4-4-0 No 62529 of Class D16/3 sets off with the 4.38pm through train to Harwich. The 'Clauds' were a proud and dignified engine in the best British 4-4-0 tradition and it is sad indeed that an example was not preserved. 2.4.59.*

86 *Earlier on the same day a Gresley B17 'Sandringham' class No 61623 'Lambton Castle' from Cambridge shed in excellent external condition prepares to make the customary cautious crossing over the wooden bridge spanning the Moreton Leam on the way out of Peterborough East. It is heading the 9.8am train from Leicester London Rd. to Cambridge via St. Ives. 2.4.59.*

87 January 17th 1959 was a dull, inhospitable day with a hard frost holding a sprinkling of snow. Here one of March's five V2s No 60928 backs on to the 10am express from Lowestoft to York. Judging from the emissions from the safety valves and chimney the fireman isn't leaving anything to chance!

88 Another local engine K3 No 61976 is given a jogging turn on the 11.40am local to Lincoln.

89 *A rather run-down and neglected B12 4-6-0 No 61575 leaking steam profusely sets out from March with the 9.8am train from Leicster London Rd. to Cambridge. 17.1.59.*

90 *A short while later a March K3 2-6-0 No 61840 drags an up freight onto the main line south of the station. 17.1.59.*

91 During a period of near total gloom when very little movement of the light meter needle was apparent a Norwich B1 No 61042 prepares to leave March with the 10.15am through train from York to Norwich and Lowestoft. 17.1.59.

92 Southbound freight was routed round the side of March station to rejoin the up main line in time to negotiate the notorious level crossing of the B1101 road. From the station footbridge a locally shedded K1 2-6-0 No 62038 heads a heavily loaded Class H freight which it has collected from nearby Whitemoor yard. 17.1.59.

Following pages

93 B17 4-6-0 No 61623 'Lambton Castle' pulls out of March with the 9.8am train from Leicester London Rd. to Cambridge via St. Ives. Driver Hipkin and his fireman who have provided some smoke effects make sure that they get into the picture. 2.4.59.

94 *The morning parcels train for Ipswich moves out of March station with B17 4-6-0 No 61637*

96 Wreathed in steam and in the shadows, a B17 4-6-0 'Honingham Hall' arrives back at March with the 10.15am express from York to Norwich and Lowestoft. 17.1.59.

97 A Doncaster V2 No 60935 makes an energetic exit from March and passes the North Junction with the morning through train from Lowestoft and Norwich to York. 2.4.59.

98 *Great Eastern Section characters. The Cambridge crew of B17 No 61623 'Lambton Castle', Driver Dennis Hipkin and his mate, pose for the camera before setting off from Peterborough East with the 9.8am train from Leicester London Rd. to Cambridge. 2.4.59.*

99 *Driver Ralph Frost from March prepares to get D1613 No 62529 on the move from March with the 1.49pm train from Cambridge to Birmingham. 2.4.59.*

100 *A flying visit to Norwich on January 14th 1961 in pursuit of the last B12 4-6-0 fortuitously co-incided with the careful grooming of 'Britannia' Pacific No 70009 'Alfred the Great' in preparation for royal duty on the 16th. With burnished buffer, polished nameplate, whitened wheel rims, brake hoses, smokebox shed and number plates every effort is being made to content*

101 *No 61572, the last surviving B12, was not in employment when I arrived in Norwich and was languishing out of steam on the engine shed ashpits. Any hope of a cab ride was therefore quickly extinguished and I had to be content*

102 *Return to Peterborough, A 'Claud' No 62589 warily approaches Moreton Leam bridge from March with the 12.45pm train from Harwich. 17.1.59.*

Peterborough North

103 *The Nene Bridges. On Sunday June 9th 1963 an A4 Pacific No 60026 'Miles Beevor' crosses the Nene viaduct with the 5.33pm stopping train from Peterborough to Kings Cross. Despite the suburban compartment stock it has charge of the A4 seems reluctant to display a local passenger headcode.*

104 On the grey and gloomy afternoon of April 26th 1963 A3 No 60066 *'Merry Hampton'* looking thoroughly neglected crosses the Nene bridge with an up express from Leeds to Kings Cross.

105 A 9F 2-10-0 No 92142 is given a bit of main line running between the expresses and hurries over the Nene bridge with an up mixed freight.

106 *A down-at-heel New England V2 No 60867 dashes into Peterborough*

107 *Fulfilling its mixed traffic role a Kings Cross V2 No 60902 heads south under easy steam over the River Nene with an up express freight.*

Following pages
108 *A Kings Cross A1 Pacific No 60158 'Aberdonian' makes a satisfying picture as she crosses the Nene with an up express from Leeds to Kings Cross.*

124 "Y6b" No. 2171 of the Norfolk & Western, a modern 2-8-8-2 type.

A wisp of steam from the safety valves suggests that her boiler pressure is well up and she is in excellent fettle. An exemplary state of affairs after such a mileage that could hardly be matched by any other class of engine.

113 A shot taken from the roof of Peterborough's power station catches Grantham A3 No 60111 'Enterprise' passing the Nene carriage sidings with the 9.40am from Kings Cross to Newcastle. Until September 1957 No 60111 was a Great Central section A3 based at Leicester and was indeed the last A3 to be transferred away before the London Midland Region took control of that route. With memories of trips on her over the London Extension still fresh (*see next high speed run below*) *the photographer...*

114 Another familiar A3, No 60039 'Sandwich' which also did a short spell at Leicester Central in 1956 is seen here working back

115 *A photograph that concentrates on the ageing process visible on the dome of former Great Central Parker N5 tank No 69293 working out its last days marshalling empty stock in the Nene carriage sidings.*

116 *A Leeds Copley Hill A1 No 60130 'Kestrel' moves out of Peterborough North station and passes beneath the Crescent bowstring girder bridge with the up 'White Rose'. August 1962.*

117 *A3 No 60105 'Victor Wild' coasts non-stop through Peterborough and passes beneath the Crescent bowstring bridge with the 9.55am express from*

118 *A4 No 60015 'Quicksilver' strikes off from Peterborough North with a 6pm*

119 *On the 15th April 1963 when this photograph was taken the writing was very much on the wall for steam over the East Coast main line. A scruffy 'top shed' V2 No 60854 makes a strident*

120 *A4 No 60034 'Lord Faringdon' makes a station stop at Peterborough*

121 *Sounding a chime whistle which has assumed a distinctly jaunty angle A4 No 60003 'Andrew K. McKosh' (that name!) roars out of Peterborough North and under the Crescent bridge on the last leg of its journey to Kings Cross with an up Leeds express.*

122 *At the north end of Peterborough North an A3 No 60109 'Hermit' makes ready to depart with the 10.20am express from Kings Cross to Leeds and Bradford.*

Driver Alf Guymer and Fireman Walsh.

subdivision and empty stock duties of the new breeds it is working on its last days of ?????????? on menial station pilot duties.

STOKE BANK

The belt of limestone country separating the Fenland rivers of the Nene and Welland near Peterborough from the Trent at Newark included the climb to Stoke summit whose unobtrusive signal box was sited exactly 100 miles from Kings Cross. This 18 mile long descent in the southbound direction was a jewel in the East Coast route's crown and was the scene of more three figure speed romps in steam days than any other stretch of railway in the country.

Representatives of nearly all the Doncaster designed Eastern Region Pacific types were recorded at over 100 miles an hour at some time or other as was the occasional 'Green Arrow'. During the last years of steam the driver of V2 No 60881 which had been newly fitted with a Kylchap double chimney was ordered by 'authority' to close his regulator down at 96 mph because his engine, celebrating its new internal freedom, was building up speed with such indecent rapidity on the descent between Little Bytham and Essendine. The command didn't prevent it reaching 101.5 mph. But it was the A4 Pacifics that will always be associated with Stoke bank and very nearly all, if not the whole class, must have reached the coveted hundred with an up express at some time during their illustrious career.

Northbound, the climb began near Helpston, 5 miles north of Peterborough, and it started in easy lifts until after shedding the influence of the River Welland at Tallington the gradient steadied at 1 in 264 through Essendine. There then followed the first of two 'breathers', a two mile length of short easier gradients and levels before trains entered on a 4½ mile stretch of 1 in 200 through Little Bytham. Another respite of 1½ miles on the approach to Corby Glen was the prelude to the final 3 mile climb at 1 in 178 to Stoke box after which the effort could be eased as the train passed through Stoke tunnel and began its descent to Grantham.

My fascination for Stoke bank was deeply rooted in childhood. I was six years old when I was taken to Essendine by a railway-minded older brother. We must have caught the train from Leicester London Rd. to Stamford and then changed stations because the memory of arriving at Essendine on the branch train from Stamford East with its C12 tank still endures as does the memory of the other C12 in the bay on the up side platform with the branch train to Bourne. To a young observer the C12s seemed a very timid engine compared with what went on on the main line.

Essendine afforded a complete fulfillment. Here was a four track stretch of railway where trains travelled through wide cuttings and over airy embankments and were visible from long distances. To a boy domiciled in a city served by the 'second grade' main lines of the Midland and Great Central routes, the 'Essendine experience' brought to life those exciting pictures in the 'Railway Magazine' of massive Gresley Pacifics with burnished hinges on their smoke box doors beaming those enigmatic smiles that instantly dissolved into a threatening leer if one studied them too closely.

Then there was the matter of colour. Compared with the somewhat restrained and conservative liveries of the other three railway companies the lined-out apple green applied to the main fleet of L.N.E.R. express locomotives was particularly refreshing and this liveliness was only heightened by the animated and sometimes delightfully absurd racehorse names that were bestowed on the early Gresley Pacifics. They added a wonderful vitality to an already inspiring mechanical creation.

Finally, the joy of the spectacle was made complete by that unforgettable sound. The triple beat roar that heralded the approach of a Pacific climbing with style and determination hauling 14, 15 or 16 coaches was always guaranteed to quicken the pulse.

Of course this was by no means all for between the 'stock' expresses came the streamliners. For a while there was a silver A4 on the 'Silver Jubilee', a blue one on the 'Coronation' and other distinguished trains like the 'Flying Scotsman' and a green one on the 'West Riding Limited'. The fast freights sported K3s and the first V2s.

A further fascination to a young enthusiast was contained in a moment of high but perplexing drama. In the midst of all the super-powered expresses the somersault signals on the up main line would be pulled off and after the usual eager wait the 'Yorkshire Pullman' would career through the station headed not by a Gresley Pacific but a beautifully turned out Ivatt Atlantic going absolutely 'hell for leather' down the gradient. It was an engine from another age but what a representative! With hindsight it is a memory that is now deeply cherished.

I was also taken to Little Bytham which involved a trip onto the M. & G.N. via Saxby Junction to the exquisite stone village of Castle Bytham. After our train had left I was treated to a leg protesting 1¾ mile walk along the single line railway to its crossing of the G.N. main line and I somehow recollect that the complaints of physical discomfort were rapidly dissipated when we came within sight and earshot of the expresses. Could it be, I wonder, that my later appetite for taking lineside liberties were first kindled during these early bouts of minor trespass?

Little Bytham station was also an open and airy spot but unlike Essendine where up expresses sped through the middle road, at Bytham the main lines ran between the island platforms with the slow roads taking the outside faces. This meant that the 'main liners' passed that much closer and were much more intimidating. Consequently, it was more difficult to take them 'all in' much less read engine names. Intimidating in a different way was the scramble back to Castle Bytham to catch the train to Melton and Leicester and not a few times did we make it to the station with only minutes to spare and in a lather of sweat and juvenile beligerence.

Later on, at the end of the war, it was to Little Bytham that I cycled in the company of teenage peers to squat on the bridges and cuttings near Careby. Here I re-acquainted with familiar Pacific and V2 friends but how jaded some of them now looked in their soot and rust-coated black livery.

The strain on the short legs of a six year old was only equalled now by the effort of pedalling 35 miles and back over the East Leicestershire and Rutland heights. As for the agonies of cycling 15 miles on a flat tyre after its split inner tube had been removed and the tyre packed with roadside grass to provide a crude cushion for the wheel rim perhaps the less said the better. This certainly happened on one occasion and provided some lasting insights into the fearsome qualities of the early Hobby Horse and Bone Shaker cycles.

Such were the memories that came flooding back when I returned to Stoke bank with a camera in the late 1950s and early 60s. My mode of travel this time was one I had perfected during His Majesty's National Service namely that of hitch hiking. The stretch of line between Stoke tunnel and Essendine was not exactly easy to reach by road and a great deal of time was consumed waiting for lifts and walking the quieter lanes. No doubt a lot of exciting photographs were missed but there was always the compensation of the surrounding spread of a particularly delightful English landscape where farming was still mixed and the stone villages still 'local'.

A new and then much repeated experience of Stoke bank was the 'driver negotiated' footplate ride between Grantham and Peterborough. I must have enjoyed scores of these in both directions on A1s, A3s, A4s and V2s. It was a V2 trip southbound from Grantham that particularly warms the memory not for any sensational running but because the weather and conditions attaching to the run created something of an ideal. The engine was 60846, an Ardsley engine with a local crew working the 10.28 Friday night Second Class only Summer train from Leeds to Kings Cross and surreptitiously I was welcomed onto the footplate at 12.50 in the morning when the train ran in.

With little 'Top Shed' finesse evident in the driving style we made a gloriously noisy climb to Stoke to emerge from the tunnel into a full moonlight that lit up the engine, tracks and landscape in a most wonderful way. When the double track at Stoke box became four and the country opened out, the sensation of surmounting the summit and commencing the descent was wonderfully conveyed by a combination of phenomena enhanced by the clarity of the moonlight. As 60846's softly lit smokebox and boiler gradually dipped to the falling gradient and its cut-off was shortened so the distant and piercing colour lights of Corby Glen came into view below us. So too did the wan and uncertain headlamps of a down sleeper whose A1 Pacific thrusting the sparks from its chimney clambered up the hill towards us offering a brief snatch of its breathy chatter as it passed with its string of coaches. It was a moment of sheer poetry that owed nothing to statistics and efficiency graphs but everything to the senses.

Watching the procession of steam hauled expresses from some of the verdant stretches of Stoke bank undoubtedly provided a most profound therapy for a great many people both young and old. The dynamic elegance, unique sound and mechanically beautiful action of the Gresley and Peppercorn engines in particular made them a stimulating spectacle that quickened the pulse. Then, after their burden of carriages had passed the senses would relax and the placid softness of a genial piece of English landscape would take over once more until the next express announced itself.

That such diversions satisfied some deep emotions there was no doubt and a touching confirmation of this was to be found not far from the station at Essendine. At a quiet spot beside the line is a small tablet remembering a young man for whom this part of Stoke bank must have held a special meaning and offered an essential refuge.

The tablet is mounted on a length of white painted bull head rail driven into the ground inside a curb of whitened stones. Within the kerb are spring flowers still tended by platelayers and lengthmen. The inscription reads:-

In Memory
of
Brian N. P. Carter
Llangunnor, Carmarthen, South Wales.
who died September 8th 1950
aged 23 years
whose mortal remains are scattered
at this spot in the
Parish of Essendine, Rutland.

Possessed of a life infirmity, which beset
his ambition to follow a career in the
Railway World, nevertheless he acquired a
wide knowledge of Railways. He frequented
this site and desired that his remains should
rest here.

Erected by his Parents and Colleagues of the
United Dairies (W) Ltd.
Carmarthen.

This little memorial does more than commemorate a tragically short life. It also bears witness to the power of that wonderful functional art form, the steam locomotive, to move, inspire and elevate the human spirit perhaps as profoundly as any music, literature and the visual arts. Indeed, out of such a force was surely born the whole preservation movement.

127 *Brian Carter's Memorial – Essendine.*

128 *A cold, wintry day in 1962 finds A4 No 60015 'Quicksilver' making brisk progress against a keen northerly wind as she passes Careby on the approach to Little Bytham with a down express from Kings Cross to Leeds.*

129 *Also approaching Little Bytham on the down slow line is Austerity 2-8-0 No 90051 with a long train of coal empties destined for Colwick yard. While the attention was captured by the scintillating traffic on the main line it was all too easy to ignore the driving skills demanded by a long, slogging, exposed climb against a hostile gale with a lengthy train of empty wagons carrying*

130 The Colwick crew of B1 No 61175 set off for home with a down freight along the slow line after exchanging trains with a New England crew at Little Bytham. The latter will work B1 No

131 A4 No 60025 'Falcon' hurries down

132 On a keen January day an A1 Pacific No 60141 'Abbotsford' sprints down the grade and

133 Climbing on the clear line with a northbound freight near the same spot a QF 2-10-0 No

135 An unidentified A1 Pacific scorches south past Little Bytham with an up express from Newcastle.

Bytham another 9F is caught climbing steadily towards Stoke summit with coal empties for Colwick yard.

136 *A dull morning in April 1960 finds a Doncaster V2 No 60817 hurrying up Stoke bank with*

137 *The driver of A1 Pacific No 60130 'Kestrel' concentrates hard on the road ahead as his*

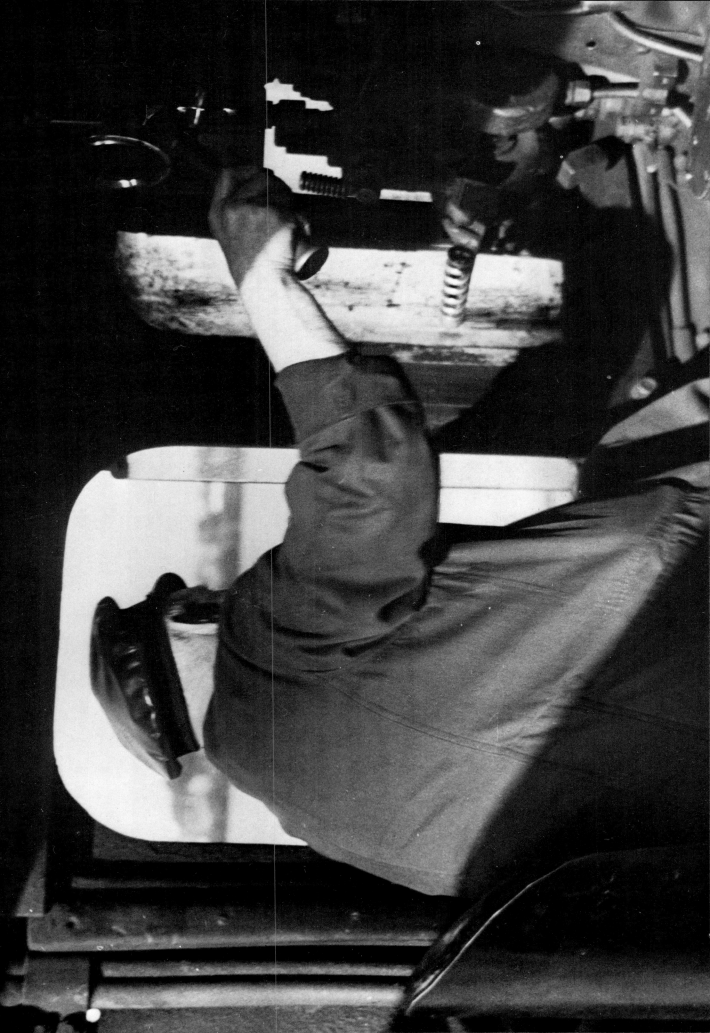

Previous pages

138 On January 19th 1963, long after the East Coast main line expresses had been taken over by the Deltics and English Electric Type 4s, I braved the arctic conditions and hitch hiked from Leicester through Stamford to Little Bytham in the hope of catching a steam loco deputising for a failed or unavailable diesel. Such occurrences were not unusual at that time. As it turned out the passenger services had settled down after the Christmas and New Year 'bulges' and with the exception of an A1 and V2 travelling down the bank on the **up with an** express and fitted freight respectively the diesels threatened to rule the day. Northbound the only sight to lift the spirits was a 9F heading a freight on the slow line until, soon after three in the afternoon as the sun was ready to slide behind the wooded skyline the 1.15pm departure from Kings Cross announced its steam haulage in no uncertain fashion. Battling against a vicious north easterly wind A4 No 60010 'Dominion of Canada' looked absolutely stunning. As it charged up the grade it left a trail of exhaust that froze and crystalised almost as soon as it left the engine's chimney to drift away over the roof tops of the village. Having waited around for over five hours in bleak conditions my feet and hands were pretty well sapped of all feeling and subzero temperatures. How I managed to hold a heavy brass camera steady and press the stiff button to fire its

139 Some free range activity near Corby Glen is momentarily disturbed by another A1 Pacific No 60146 'Peregrine' which is standing down State bank with its hel.

140 *An A3 No 60067 'Ladas' climbs past the same spot with a down Leeds express. 11.8.62.*

141 *On the same day an A4 Pacific No 60033 'Seagull' with the*
'Yorkshire Pullman' begins to take on the speed between Gantley

143 *A Grantham A3 No 60106 'Flying Fox' heading an up relief express from Newcastle to Kings Cross exchanges greetings on Stoke bank with stablemate No 60048 'Doncaster' which is climbing finely with an express from Kings Cross to York and Hull.*

144 *Passing Stoke summit in good spirits with the down 'Queen of Scots' Pullman is A1 No 60123 'H. A. Ivatt'.*

145 *It was common practice on the G.N. main line to sometimes put a big engine on stopping trains to Peterborough and Grantham for reasons of operating convenience. The engine would return to London on an up express. Here, A4 No 60003 'Andrew K. McKosh' whisks the 10.40am 'Parly' from Kings Cross to Grantham past Stoke summit. 12.4.60.*

146 *The up 'Norseman' express from Newcastle to Kings Cross speeds out of the south end of Stoke Tunnel hauled by A4 No 60006 'Sir Ralph Wedgewood'. 12.4.60.*

7.53am from Sunderland to Kings Cross. No 60112 is wearing the small smoke deflector shields that were fitted after its rebuilding with a Kylchap double blast pipe. They were not very effective in lifting the exhaust and soon gave way to the German trough type deflectors.

of Stoke Tunnel with the down 'White Rose'. 12.4.60.

149 A 'top shed' A3 No 60107 'Royal Lancer' approaches Stoke Tunnel at High Dyke with a

150 A 9F No 92198 with a mixed freight joins the up main line at High Dyke after being held on

151 *From the down side of the main line A4 No 60022 'Mallard' is caught speeding out of Stoke tunnel with the down 'Flying Scotsman'. 12.4.60.*

HIGH DYKE

There was something rather odd about the discovery of a single track standard gauge railway line tracing its way through the pastoral uplands and past some of the serene limestone villages of the Rutland – Lincolnshire border well removed from the main lines and established passenger routes.

Laid over the surface of a landscape which gave to it a distinct switchback profile with frequent changes of gradient, some as steep as 1 in 40, it had all the characteristics of a light railway with a promise of lightweight engines until one heard the strong, uneven, triple exhaust beat of a heavy, three cylinder locomotive being worked hard under load.

Such was the High Dyke branch which left the East Coast main line at the north end of the Stoke tunnel, five miles south of Grantham to push its tentacle for nearly six miles over the Great North Road at Colsterworth to the open cast workings near Stainby and Sproxton where the draglines stripped the overburden and shovels scooped up the ironstone and shovelled it into tippler wagons.

The locomotives were the Gresley 02 2-8-0s which monopolised the working of the branch during the last years of steam and which after trials with a number of different engine types were found to be the most suitable on account of their superior tractive effort combined with the starting and slow speed advantages of three cylinder small wheel drive.

The 'Tangos' came from Grantham shed as did their crews for whom a turn of duty on the branch was dubbed, perhaps for obvious reasons, "going into the Alps". Because of the line's peculiarities some unique strategies, improvisations and 'dodges' were employed which were not to be found in the rule book. The severity and abrupt changes of gradient, the scarcity of passing places, the opening of crossing gates by train crews and the weight and 'stretch' of loose-coupled wagons all contributed to some ad hoc methods of operation. There was a consensus view on the part of the branch staff that if all the regulations had been strictly observed it would have been difficult if not impossible to work it.

The branch was controlled by electric tablet between High Dyke and Skillington Road and six of the O2s were fitted with special tablet catchers similar to those used on the Somerset and Dorset though latterly they were little used. Beyond Skillington Road where the lines to Stainby and Sproxton parted, train staff was used. The official load limits were set at 18 tipplers full and 40 empty, though again this was one of the rules that was occasionally 'bent'.

As most of the worst climbs were encountered outward bound from High Dyke it was customary to take the empties onto the branch engine first so that loaded trains came back tender leading. This was possibly a safety measure which ensured that the water in the long boilers of the O2s would be concentrated at the firebox end when they tackled the steepest inclines.

Riding a run down 'Tango' tender-first heaving a full load plus(!) of ironstone up the 1 in 60 out of the Colsterworth 'dip' and over the Great North Road on full regulator and in full back gear was a rugged pleasure indeed! It was not just the din but the quite sickening thud that jarred right through the engine each time the worn big ends came over. Those engines certainly took some punishment but they did the work and with a crew who understood them they did it well.

While waiting for expresses on the main line at Stoke tunnel it was always fascinating to observe the ritual that was enacted by loaded trains of ore when they came off the branch. At the top of the 1 in 40 descent to the main line the 'Tango', running tender first, would have to stop at the fixed distant signal while the guard wandered down the train pinning down half the wagons' brakes. The train would then cautiously descend further and stop again on the curving gradient so that the guards van could be unhooked after its brake had been applied. This done, the engine would take the loaded tipplers into one of the reception sidings north of the signal box leaving the brake van behind on the bank.

Once the train was safely 'inside', the points would be changed and the brake van, with the assistance of gravity, would run down and be directed into the other empty reception siding where it would be brought to a smart stop by the guard before it collided with the buffer stops at the end. It was then ready for another trip up the branch behind some more empties. The final manoeuvre saw the propelling of the loaded tipplers from the reception road into the departure sidings alongside the main line exit from Stoke tunnel after which the O2 was also ready for its next assignment.

The ore brought out along the High Dyke branch was of the Northampton Sand variety with an iron content when dry of around 40%. Over the years it was extracted from open cast 'mines' at Colsterworth, Colsterworth Glebe, Stainby, Cringle and Sproxton many of which had been owned and worked since the 1920s by the Appleby-Frodingham Steel Company at Scunthorpe and the Rotherham based Parkgate Iron and Steel Company. After the nationalisation of the steel industry most of the ore from High Dyke still continued to feed their respective furnaces.

When steam operation came to an end in 1963 there were still seven loaded trains each weekday from High Dyke to Frodingham running loose coupled under class 8 headlamps. The returning empties were condensed into six trains and motive power was usually an 'Austerity' 2-8-0 or an O2 from Grantham shed.

One train a day was despatched to the former Parkgate works at Aldwarke near Rotherham and this was particularly interesting because it was a class 4 fully fitted express freight running on the main line to Doncaster Bridge Junction where it was turned onto the Sheffield line, At its destination it collected the previous day's empties and returned via Tinsley East and Darnall West junctions to rejoin the G.N. main line at Retford. The 'Aldwarke job' was given VIP treatment and its haulage was normally entrusted to a Pacific.

The regular ironstone traffic from High Dyke was concluded by two trains a day to Colwick bound for the steel works at Stanton.

For a time after the steam era the future of the High Dyke branch looked quite rosey when a seam of high grade ore was discovered below ground close to the branch at Burton Crossing and the Easton drift mine was sunk to procure it. Alas, nature intervened when an underground water course was breached and the workings became flooded to the point where pumps were unable to cope with the ingress. The mine was eventually abandoned to become the site of a huge food refrigeration plant which welcomed a plentiful supply of on-site water.

The light engine movements and working of empties from the main line into High Dyke sidings was always something of an operational headache involving as it did the blocking of both up and down main lines while the manoeuvre was undertaken. Had the branch survived it is unlikely that such an arrangement could have continued after electrification and some other strategy would have had to be devised to remove the obstruction.

The importation of cheaper, high grade iron ore with a reduced lime and phosphorus content via the north eastern ports spelt the demise of the indigenous iron stone industry and all the workings in the English Midlands came to an end in 1980. Local reserves in the area, however, are still considerable but for the forseeable future it would seem to be more economical to feed our much reduced modern furnace capacity with ore from Canada, Brazil, Spain and West Africa than to use native bedded brands. Perhaps one day if foreign supplies run out or become too expensive to ship-in, the High Dyke branch might be revived and the whole operation restarted. Unlikely perhaps, but who knows?

Following pages **152** *Even a 'Tango' could look proud. Having recently returned from a general overhaul at Doncaster works a Grantham 02 No 63933 waits to leave High Dyke sidings with a train load of ironstone for Frodingham steel works.*

153 *On the last day of steam working over the High Dyke branch on September 7th 1963 a Grantham 02 No 63940 climbs the 1 in 40 away from High Dyke with a train of empty tipplers bound for Stainby sidings.*

154 *Later the same day the crew of 'Tango' No 63932 put up a rousing display as they tackle the stiff climb.*

155 *In the wintry conditions of February 1962 02 No 63932 climbs the 1 in 40 away from High Dyke and passes beneath the farm occupation bridge with a train of ironstone empties.*

156 *A shot from the cab of 02 No 63931 approaching the same bridge shows the steep climb stretching ahead of the engine.*

159 'The Aldwarke Job'. A variation from the sequence of High Dyke ironstone trains to Frodingham in North Lincolnshire was the daily fitted, or 'express', stone train to the former Parkgate Iron & Steel Company's works at Aldwarke near Rotherham. This train ran main line under a Class 4 headcode to Doncaster Bridge Junction where it turned off for Rotherham. The engine then picked up the previous day's empties and returned to the G.N. main line via Tinsley East and Darnall West Junctions to Retford. On a weekday after leaving High Dyke soon after 6.30pm the engine was back with its train of empties by 2am. In its last years it was retimed to leave High Dyke on Saturdays soon after 2pm.

160 It is the 16th February 1963 and A3 No 60046 'Diamond

Northern in 1945 was an insensitive professional blunder and amongst other shortcomings the result was visually lacking in elegance. Here, No 60113 'Great Northern' climbs past High Dyke with the 12.20pm express from Hull to Kings Cross. 19.4.62.

an up class D freight. 25.3.61.

5.10pm from Newcastle to Kings Cross was taken from the flat concrete roof of the shunters cabin below the signal box shown in a previous photograph. Unfortunately, the exciting sound of the approaching train coincided with the more ominous one of the shunter re-charging his stove with coal and as the A4 appeared so did the smoke from the stove chimney which wafted across the lens of the camera at the crucial moment. The language around High Dyke on a summer evening could be quite rich!

164 A1 Pacific No 60145 'Saint Mungo' confidently hustles the up 'Yorkshire Pullman' beneath the gantry controlling the approach to High Dyke. 25.3.61.

165 *From near the same spot A3 No 60065 'Knight of Thistle' romps up the climb from Grantham to Stoke with the 12.20pm*

166 *An old favourite No 60103 'Flying Scotsman' in 'unmodernised' form roars up the climb to Great Ponton with an express*

167 *From the cab window an A1 Pacific No 60130 'Kestrel' is seen approaching the gantry at High Dyke with the up 'White Rose'. Up on the embankment an 02 pauses after working in from Stainby with ironstone August 1962.*

168 *Running 5 minutes ahead of time A4 No 60012 'Commonwealth of Australia' approaches Great Ponton with the up 'Elizabethan'.*

169 A King's Cross A1 No No 60139 'Sea Eagle' climbs confidently up Stoke bank and approaches Great Ponton with an up

170 In the cold, brittle sunshine of a winter day in January 1961 a Leeds Copley Hill A1 Pacific No 60134 'Foxhunter' makes a dynamic picture as she climbs Stoke bank between Grantham and

by A3 No 60109 'Hermit' shortly after the engine had been fitted with trough type smoke deflectors. She is seen dashing down the gradient towards Grantham.

outstandingly successful engine was further improved was that the original Gresley design was not a final statement but was so advanced that there was still scope for inexpensive but significant improvement throughout their distinguished career. Such a virtue was not possessed by that many British express passenger and mixed traffic types where improvement could only be achieved by extensive and costly rebuilding. How sad that the V2s received the Kylchap treatment at the end of their days and how perfect they would have been for the Edinburgh – Aberdeen and Waverley routes. Also, what would Leicester Central men have done with them on the 'Master Cutler'?! Ah well, we shall never know but here is No 60902 making leisurely work of climbing Stoke bank with a southbound fitted freight.

away from Granham and crosses the Witham and on up Leeds express.

GRANTHAM

The Lincolnshire town of Grantham was the nearest railway centre on the G.N. main line to my home in Leicester and until December 7th 1953 it was possible to take the somewhat indirect but delightful train service from Leicester Belgrave Road to Grantham via Marefield Junction, Melton Mowbray and Bottesford.

It was an attractively rural journey of 40¼ miles taking an hour and a half and calling at 13 stations unless one travelled on the 'express' which was impudently and quite successfully put on by the Eastern Region in 1950 to entice passengers away from the rival London Midland's 'Thames Clyde Express'. With only three station stops it contrived to do the journey in an hour and eleven minutes and made a most convenient connection with the down 'Flying Scotsman'.

By Lincolnshire Road Car or Birmingham and Midland Motor Omnibus the journey time for the 30 main road miles was also 1½ hours.

When its railway was dominated by steam Grantham possessed a number of attractive features. It boasted a celebrated engine shed and the town was an important staging point for engines on many of the expresses. Unlike other depots on the G.N. main line however, which were usually to be found well away from the stations. Grantham's shed was located alongside the station so that in the lulls between expresses on the main line one had the bonus of watching individual and often renowned engines moving around the shed yard displaying their elegance as they prepared for or concluded their duties.

For those with an addiction for entering the prohibited reserve of the engine shed it was usual to leave the station and make for the narrow pedestrian tunnel that passed beneath the tracks and platforms thus affording subterranean acess to the shed yard gate.

Apart from its own allocation of notable engines Grantham also played host to visitors from Kings Cross, Doncaster, Leeds, York and Newcastle and this provided a good mix of Pacifics covering A1s, A2s, A3s and the 'streamliners' together with those fine looking 'reservists' the V2s.

As Peter Handford's inspired recordings at Grantham reveal so well the enthusiast congregations that collected at the platform ends were likewise treated to the whole symphony of three cylinder sound not just from engines re-starting trains from the station but also from light engine movements. Those working south to Kings Cross having turned, watered and coaled up would leave the shed yard tender first and join the up main line beyond the North signal box. They would then return and pass through the station with steam shut off on their way to the engine siding at the south end. The big Gresley engines would do so to the accompaniment of that unforgettable "lank-mm-ber-lonk" that resonated from the rods and valve gear with each revolution of the driving wheels. It was a strong, confident sound that was intensely pleasing to one pair of ears.

Grantham was also different from other centres on the G.N. main line most of which seemed to be situated on low or flat ground under the influence of a mature river. Instead, the town was in a stone belt and this made for some interesting settings in which to photograph steam.

Dominated by the soaring proportions of its parish church spire, Grantham's skyline was happily 'set off' by the gently rolling limestone heights surrounding it and once the embanked railway had left the proximity of the junior River Witham the hills closed in to create those undulating cuttings leading to the tunnels north and south of the town at Peasecliffe and Stoke.

I found the wide cutting on the down side beyond the Great North Road bridge near Saltersford a particularly rewarding spot because from any height it gave a broad, unrestricted view onto the railway. Equally important, its vegetation was sufficiently short and 'soft' and its slope shallow enough for a large measure of upholstered comfort to be enjoyed when reclining during the waits between trains. On a warm summer day the relaxation it bestowed was profound indeed.

Like Kings Cross, Grantham also possessed for me its share of high adrenalin episodes. Among these was a somewhat reckless attempt I made one summer night in 1958 to achieve two unofficial 'blind' footplate runs to Kings Cross and back.

My first round trip going up on No 60014 'Silver Link' and returning with home based A1 No 60122 'Curlew' was accomplished without difficulty. However, as I was wandering down to the engine siding to negotiate my second trip to London on No 60800 'Green Arrow' which was waiting for its train a vigilant member of the station staff spotted me and raised a most vociferous challenge. The gist of his outburst was that he had seen me earlier installing myself on the A4.

At 3.30 in the morning I had little stomach for a rowdy interrogation and swiftly decided that it would be prudent to abandon my second trip and beat a rapid retreat. A most undignified pursuit ensued along the narrow alleyways through the nearby estate of railway terraces which eventually seemed to involve several station personnel and a BTC policeman!

Crossing the main Melton road in the dark I managed to take refuge under a bridge over the stream that runs below the railway viaduct. After an anxious spell of activity during which hurried footsteps passed overhead and a voice shouted "I think he went that way" the chase must have been called off and some composure was recovered.

Unfortunately, there had been no opportunity to wash off the abundant grime accumulated during my two footplate trips and this ruled out any chance of hitching an early lift back to Leicester. I was therefore left with the prospect of waiting for the first bus which didn't leave Grantham until 6.30 am. So, on a gloriously warm summer morning as the sun came up I settled down in the long grass beside the stream and slept the sleep of the wicked oblivious even to the sound of trains crossing the viaduct above me.

When it was time to set foot on the main road, great caution was required because 6 am was a change of shift at the station and I might still have been spotted. A bus stop was sought that was well clear of the railway and when the Lincoln green of double decker service No 25 to Melton Mowbray and Leicster approached the sigh of relief was unrestrained and very audible.

I well understood the looks of suspicion that greeted my entry onto the bus and the perplexity with which I was eyed by the conductor when I purchased my ticket. I could not have presented a very pretty sight!

Another moment of acute embarrassment is recalled by the photograph taken from the cab of A3 No 60106 'Flying Fox' on its way down Stoke bank with No 60048 approaching. 'Flying Fox' was the first A3 I ever footplated on when she was working over the Great Central section from Leicester Central and as I was not then in possession of a camera I was unable to record the event.

No 60106 held a special interest for me, so, after she had returned to the G.N. section and become a Grantham engine, I endeavoured to put right the ommission. However, for one reason or another my efforts were not too successful until one Saturday in early autumn 1962 when I was completing a day's lineside photography and preparing a weary return home to Leicester she unexpectedly appeared in the up engine siding having been booked at short notice to work forward an extra from Newcastle to Kings Cross. On the spur of the moment I decided to approach her driver, Arthur Northern, who I had never previously met, and begged a trip to London. He readily agreed and donning my overalls and grease cap I happily joined him and his fireman.

It was not until we were running down Holloway Bank into the terminus that I realised that I had insufficient money to pay for a train ticket from St. Pancras to Leicester and so had to borrow a 10 shilling note from a man who was still, more or less, a stranger. He not only received his 10 shillings back by return of post but also a batch of very appreciative photographs when they were eventually printed.

As Grantham will be the point of departure for Part Two of 'Eastern Region Steam Twilight' I have confined the material in this book to traffic working south of the town. Northbound trains and shots around the engine shed will therefore provide the opening to Part Two which will continue down the G.N. main line to Doncaster with a pause at Retford and will include diversions short, long and prolonged into Skegness, Nottingham and Lincoln.

175 *An overcast afternoon in August sees A4 No 60016 'Silver King' being fired for the climb to Stoke after passing Grantham with an up non-stop express from Newcastle to Kings Cross.*

176 *A K3 2-6-0 No 61867 heads south along the main line under easy steam with an up fitted freight.*

177 *A 9F 2-10-0 No 92175 with a down mixed freight which* includes 16 fitted vans of inspect

engine climbs away through the Grantham suburbs along the up slow line with a mixed freight.

through the Saltisford cutting with a down fitted train of containers. In the background the glorious spire of St. Wulfram's parish church rises from the centre of the town.

180 *An A4 Pacific No 60010 'Dominion of Canada' sets off from Grantham*

182 After being checked by signals on the way down Stoke bank with a down Newcastle express, A3 No 60061 'Pretty Polly' makes an impatient recovery as it passes through the Saltisford cutting on its way into Grantham. April 1962.

shamefaced into Grantham with a long train of coal empties bound for Colwick yard. Judging by the streamliner's condition it has only just emerged from a general overhaul at Doncaster works and is being given some gentle running in before returning to express duty. 14.6.62.

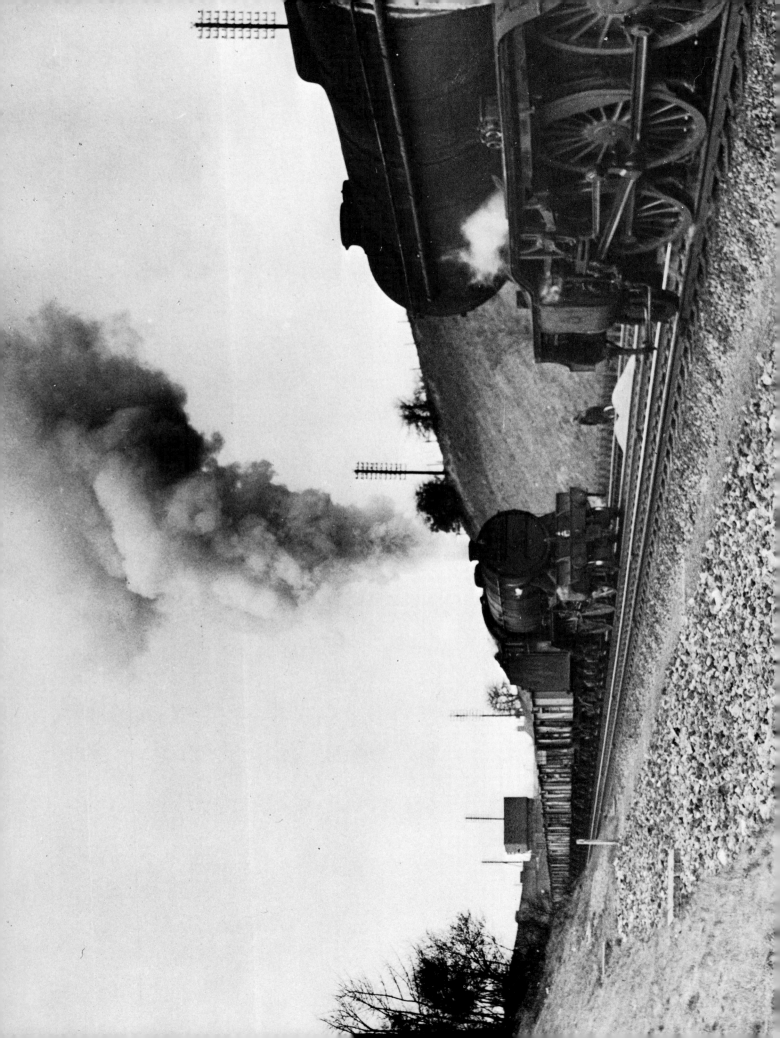

Saltisford cutting on the way to Stoke tunnel with the 2.45pm express from Hull to Kings Cross. 24.4.62.

Saltisford cutting at Grantham and passes V2 No 60925 which is entering the town with a down train of empty stock.

185 A3 Pacific No 60049 'Galtee More' from Grantham depot gets into its stride as it tackles the climb to Stoke with the 12.45pm express from Hull to Kings Cross. 9.6.62.

186 A Grantham O2 No 63931 takes a train of ironstone empties from Frodingham to High Dyke along the up slow line in Saltisford cutting. The bridge it has passed under carries the Great North

187 Another A1 No 60131 'Osprey' is going well as it scurries up Stoke bank after passing through Grantham non-stop with a relief to the up 'White Rose'. 24.4.62.

188 A photograph which is a reminder that the best laid schemes could sometimes go woefully wrong. On Saturday September 8th 1962 when I was loitering with intent around the station area at Grantham I observed A4 No 60025 'Falcon' in the yard siding waiting to take over an up Newcastle express. She looked very good and there was a hazy sun so I arranged a smoke with the crew and described the spot where I would photograph them. My intention was to take the A4 in the Saltisford cutting as it was going away from the camera and to catch it as it passed between two young silver birch trees that were in the foreground of my picture. Alas, what I did not consider was the effect of a fresh north easterly breeze. When 'Falcon' appeared with a magnificent exhaust I suddenly realised that the smoke was being blown rapidly across to the bank where I was standing and that it was nearly keeping pace with the train. If, therefore, I allowed the engine to reach the 'right' spot so that it was nicely positioned between the two trees the smoke would have caught up and the photograph would be ruined. So, in desperation, I had to fire the shutter early and not a split second before time because the moment I did so both frames and [...]

189 No 60044 'Melton' again. Soon after it had been fitted with a Kylchap double chimney, 'Melton' is seen opening up for the climb to Stoke with the 7.50am from Newcastle to Kings Cross.

190 What an ideal way to spend a summer afternoon! Four schoolboys have their attention riveted by A3 No 60061 'Pretty Polly' as it draws out of Grantham with the 10.52am from . . .

192 A1 Pacific No 60115 'Meg Merrilies' passes the same spot with an up express from Newcastle.

North Road having passed Grantham non-stop with a relief express from York to Kings Cross.

chimney, is photographed from the Great North Road bridge climbing away through the Saltisford cutting with an up express from Leeds to Kings Cross.

appeared on the station banning tram spotters it is interesting to see the two schoolboys complete with satchels and notebooks discreetly tucked round the corner by the yard box out of the sight of 'authority'. In a modern age of soccer violence and teenage ferment what a wholesome and harmless interest the railway offered to an earlier generation.

195 *The Great North Road bridge was a recurrent image in my photographs at Grantham. In this one A4 No 60013 'Dominion of New Zealand' dives beneath it with an express from Hull and Doncaster to Kings Cross.*

196 *Grantham's A3 No 60106 'Flying Fox' gathers speed away from the town as she climbs Stoke bank with the 12.45pm express from Hull to Kings Cross.*

'Northumbrian': 7.9.57.

press camera case and holdall containing my footplate overalls and hat can be seen beside the waiting cyclist at the bottom of the platform ramp.

202 *Getting towards the end of its regular service A4 No 60022 'Mallard' arrives in Grantham with the 10.35am from Newcastle to Kings Cross and quickly gathers an admiring audience.*

203 *In spite of a drenching shower a Kings Cross V2 No 60871 obviously means business as it waits impatiently beside the yard signal box at the end of the up platform with the Friday 4pm express from Darlington to Kings Cross. 21.4.62.*

204 *A final picture that perhaps fully captures the G.N. main line big engine departure. Locally shedded A3 No 60049 'Galtee More' roars into life as she momentarily picks up her feet and slips while pulling out with the 10.50am express from Leeds to Kings Cross. 11.8.62.*